Didicoy
Karen Downs-Barton

smith|doorstop

the poetry business

Published 2023 by
Smith|Doorstop Books
The Poetry Business
Campo House,
54 Campo Lane,
Sheffield S1 2EG

ISBN 978-1-914914-37-9
Typeset by Utter
Printed by People for Print

Smith|Doorstop Books are a member of Inpress:
www.inpressbooks.co.uk

Distributed by NBN International, 1 Deltic Avenue,
Rooksley, Milton Keynes MK13 8LD

The Poetry Business gratefully acknowledges the support of
Arts Council England.

Supported by
ARTS COUNCIL
ENGLAND

Contents

Hamime: My Mixed Language is My Mixed Identity
A Coupling with Henry Mayhew after Karen MacCarthy Woolf

The cant or slang of the patterer is not the cant of the costermonger, but
    my Romani tongue, a wayside patrin of twigs and leaves, rustles

a system of its own. As in the case of the costers, it is interlarded
    with secrets on bitti-barvals from distant shores. Scattered

with general remarks,
    traces of the Indic spark its musika-hamima

while ordinary language is so smothered,
    within the dominant vernacular, its patois, mother-tongue,

so subdued, that unless when professionally engaged
    weaving tales of a Romani family

and talking of their wares,
    their transient lives where only Romani blood ties

they might almost pass for foreigners.
    because travellers are foreigners everywhere.

Patrin (pateran): Romani wayside signs made from leaves and twigs, also leaf, or pages of a book depending on context. **Hamime**: fused, blended, adulterated, as in hamimé-ratêsko, mixed blood. **Bitti barvals**: breezes. **Gry**: horse.

Framed By Wood Grain

i

After the shock of discovery, the police
arrive, an ambulance must come and go, leaving
space where his body had been. Neighbours you never
liked gather outside watching the soap opera, say
Well, what do you expect with their sort in the road?
You become a rag doll; blank face stitched with button
eyes, fixed on the empty sag of his chair, the gap
at the table where his head had been. You question

But did I see him breathing? In stillness you hear
a train rush in your ears, feel your palms as prickles.
A bottle throws rainbows at the wall. Everything
is more-so, except him. You don't speak, your mother
has left her cotton body, its stale sweat mixing
with mock orange, his gift of perfume, *Je Reviens.*

ii

Aunties come, just lift the latch, and walk in.
They bring food on plates with tin foil covers,
and bulbous pans of rice and peas. Their dish cloth
shrouds trail steamy clouds across bammy moons.
They can't see your mother is a cloth doll
propped in her corner, try to busy her.
Old men bring rum and dominoes, mutter
This curried goat surely tastes like mutton.

Everyone has a role, known and gendered
but you are invisible watching them
move furniture till the little room looks
like a stranger's room where you don't belong.
No matter how your table shifts or fills
the head that laid there still haunts button eyes.

iii

Dominoes slap wood as Marley sings. The talk
is of Windrush tinged with recent scandals.
Desmond questions if the body should be laid out
here or with the married wife. Plates clatter. The game
continues. *Some men just can't handle their affairs.*
A fly is shushed out the window. You think about
that other family and wonder if they know
about the knotted head on your table. You're sent

with older girls to the bedroom where you learn how
to turn the mattress so a duppy won't trouble
your mother's pregnant body. Sitting together
on the candlewick coverlet, not reading just
watching the paraffin heater's blue flame dancing,
you feel the pain of being stitched back together.

A Confluence of Reds and Silks

1. **Lalli,** *adj.* red (your tongue translates it as a song started) *la-lliii*
   Par, *n.* silk (you hear it as diaphanous, a breathiness) *pahrr*

my mother's *lalli* scarf   a wet cherry colour   slips untied   floats
like *toof* like smoke   from her hair   strokes her shoulder   drifts
floorward wreaths   her naked foot   with a sigh of *par*

2. **Ranchkia,** *adj.* red (your tongue translates as a lariat of call and response) *rans-ki-eh*
   Keski, *n.* silk (your ear hears it as dropped glass exploding) *kes-kiii*

brushing her hair   100 strokes   her mantra '*keski,   keski*'
light slicks *ranchkia* highlights   the Indic garnets   in strands of jet
in the mirror   someone's hands coil   a plaited milk snake   about her head

3. **Allulo,** *adj.* red (your tongue translates as ululations) *a-llu-low*
   Paranni, *n.* silk (your ear hears as a perfume atomised to sound) *paranneee*

she is alluring in his favourite dress Mandarin collar
allulo heels and lips   the whisper   of *parrani* stockings
as she teeters   lighting candles   round his coffin

4. **Lalla,** *adj.* red (your tongue   an interlude) *la-llaaa*
   Keshano, *n.* silk (your ear hears as a rumpling falling away) *kesha-no*

tonight there will be no lullabies   she will sleep alone
in *lalla* underwear   crushed *keshano*   their cinnabar
will keep his *muller* from troubling   her slumbers

5. **Ral,** *adj.* red (your tongue interprets as a drum roll, an outro) ***rrrral***
   Rup, *n.* silk (your ear hears it as a tearing, running to a tip) ***rrrup***

when her waters rupture   Mum gives me a sister   a 'run duppy' chord
of *ral rup* tied about her finger   a safekeeping talisman
from the *mullerdi*   the ghost-father   my sister   never knew

A Love of Flesh

The morning after a night-caller
Mum would pay the rent
and put cash in the meter.
We'd have crusty rolls
from the corner shop
that filled the flat
with the yeasty warmth
of just-baked bread.
Divvying them between us,
she'd cut each cob, showering flakes,
then slather them in butter.
Sitting with a quart of prawns before her,
Mum would peel their chitin skins
like translucent baby toenails,
suck clustered orange eggs
from their abdomens,
shuck their bearded heads
to sip their brains
of salty thoughts,
then tuck their naked bodies
into the beds of our waiting rolls:
saline, sweet, and yielding.

My Mother's Professional Rituals

The stealthy filling of a tiny handbag,
brown faux crocodile,
the snap of its gold clasp.

Wads of clean tissues folded
and tucked into a sleeve or draped
in a flaccid fan at her waistband.

Her hand dipping beneath a leopard skin blouse,
tucking the crackle of small packets
into the sling for her ample breasts.

Before leaving, her glance at the mirror
where whatever was reflected never pleased
but sometimes arrested her.

At the threshold, checking her keys, calling:
Put yourself to bed. I'm off
pulling pints for the hoi polloi.

The covert reception of a night visitor: my wooden toybox
dragged across the living room door like an outsized bolt.
Inside, the urgency of muffled noises.

A man's voice mumbling as he leaves the flat.
The slap of hand on hide. The door closing
on his retreating footsteps.

Her elongated shadow falling
from my bedroom door. Shallow breathing.
Never confronting my ruse of sleep.

Echoes from the bathroom:
Gargle. Spit,
Gargle. Spit.

The running of a bath. Badedas. The medicinal scent
blending with patchouli and wet pine. The bathroom
a sound box reverberating her profanities:

You shit. You cunt. You whore.

Of the Men who Came as Shadows in the Night

i

I didn't tell you
that I remember
splinters
of your father
his charry skin   fingers
with nails of polished wood
his Calypsos and dark beauty
how on Palace Road
I played with his children

I did not say I remember him
as a form brewing
beyond stained glass   his threats
or entreaties while he taught our door
to buck against its hinges
his unhinged kicking   shouldering   lasting and lasting
before disappearing
into the black silence
of his lost battles

why conjecture about his
imploded world
the wife and sons who left him
or the role our mother played   you
growing inside her
but I told you
that you were wanted
that's the thing
you should remember

ii

Did Mum tell you
about your near
abduction?

How a man
she'd just finished with sent
strangers to our home

the echo of their knock
– just as others
knocked –

her screams as they
pushed their way in
grabbed you from the crib

I saw her desperate, fighting,
shouting you weren't his kid
I remember wondering

why no one came for me.

iii

Do you remember the stealthy men
that knocked at night, whispered negotiations,
the metal rasp as the chain slid, the door opened. Or when they
slipped that other world to shadow our days?

They worked in shops Mum scurried past,
leered from corners, or spilt
like stale beer from pub doorways. Some spat
remarks, she'd do her best to explain away.

And always, at that stage,
we'd move on
to some fresh place, new start, that was the start
of the same knocks, same remarks, just recycled.

There'd be a new home, better or worse than the last,
a new school, friends to make, and a new name
to grow into, memorised to get it right
on textbooks. Mum would wait at new school gates

never quite fitting in
but trying. Once, a policeman picking up children,
laughed, said he almost didn't recognise her
with her clothes on.

And when she said, 'Not in front of my girls.' I knew
we'd be moving again. We were always
running away from
something.

Arriving at the Home for Crying Children

'The true answer is the wrong answer.'
  – Joelle Taylor

(Ring the correct answer. More than one may apply.)

I arrived at my first local authority institution
  a. With a social worker holding files of papers. Frowning. Scary.
  b. In a police car. I'm not sure why police were involved.
  c. I can't remember. I slough memories too heavy to carry.

My little sister was
  a. Held by the policeman, her arms flapping like wings.
  b. Carried by a social worker who'd called Mum a gypo.
  c. Stuck to me like a conjoined twin, toothlessly smiling.

My sister made noises like
  a. Granddad's pigeon loft, when he strangled a squab.
  b. An old man's breathing at his end-of-days.
  c. Leaves in a storm as she wheezed through snot.

I didn't hold anyone's hand because
  a. They were strangers and I didn't trust them.
  b. I'd been sick in the car and my hands were acrid.
  c. I was holding a carrier bag of possessions.

I contemplated running away by
  a. Retracing the route to our camp in a stolen police car.
  b. Waiting till nightfall, climbing out of a window.
  c. Grabbing my sister, though she couldn't walk far.

I had to get home because
a. When my *fowki* moved-on I'd never find them.
b. My Mum needed help as her mind had got lost.
c. Trying to speak *gadje*, my tongue just fumbled.

At the House for Crying Children, we were met by
a. The smell of TCP and lots of nurses
b. A uniformed Matron though no one was ill
c. Staring children who'd lost their happiness.

The people inside
a. Took my sister although she was yelling.
b. Gave me a cupcake with crunchy sprinkles.
c. Told me I was a baby for crying.

They took my sister
a. To a room called 'Hatchlings' with blank walls and cots in rows.
b. Down winding steps where a nurse chain-smoked cigarettes.
c. Where I wasn't allowed, but heard her crying as distant echoes.

I was told
a. You ought to feel grateful for your nice new home.
b. Your Mum can visit when she's feeling better.
c. Cheer up. Say goodbye to the nice policeman.

Mageripen: The Rules of Hygiene

i.

In state children's homes, clothes you arrived in
are taken away for washing and you
might never see them again. The prefects
collect clothes in plastic baskets, ovals
big enough to take a ride in, skidded
across the linoleum landing. Boys
force each other's sweaty heads into piles
of knickers, scolded by laughing nurses.
New children who ask after their own clothes
are teased with tales of gifts to jumble sales,
burnings in boilers. But if you are sent
to the caretakers' office he'll let you
watch machines churn clothes in greyed water, spot
your waving jumper and kicking trousers.

ii

Your waving jumper and kicking trousers
decorate bushes far from each other.
A windy wash day beside Nans *vardo.*
You learn what a *Romani chai* should know:
separate clothes by body parts, top half
in white bowls, bottom half in blue, sprinkle
fistfuls of snowflake soap, swirl water to
blizzards. Scrub, wring, rinse, wring. This *mokerdi*
lore shapes rituals of cleaning. Nan's bowls are
emptied according to function. Cleaner
water near kitchen shrubs where fennel, mint

or lavender are gathered, bottom half
water is slushed in ditches, raw hands washed
to touch the bunched clothes, cleaned of their grey swill.

iii

To touch the bunched clothes, washed in their grey swill,
the caretaker uses callipers, hoiks
steamy meshed arms, legs, bodies to tumble
dry. Mist sighs from a drooping proboscis
hanging at a part-opened window. Fust
lingers on clothing, skin. I imagine him
as a dung beetle with pincer mandibles
rolling shit-ball clothes. Under the motto
Personal Possessions Breed Discontent
I practise the pretence of interest
in the wonders of his washing machines.
I'm looking for the clothing I arrived in.
It won't be stealing. No one here wants
to wear clothes worn by a 'dirty Gypsy'.

Vardo: Romani caravan. Usually settled families kept a vardo for family use or
travelling to seasonal work. *Magiripen* or *Mokerdi*: terms for Romani hygiene rules.

Dear Faye,

ask me
about the day we were caught stealing
in auntie Barbara's dining room
her posh flat on Streatham Hill

ask me
about our guilt
as horrified faces peered under
the lace edged tablecloth
and saw an open box
of dog biscuits
between us

ask me
about the bone shapes
that smelt of Farley's Rusks
arranged in coloured rows
on paper doilies

the pinks were a disappointment
like blown rose
petals
the blacks etched our teeth and tastebuds
with the grit of fire grate
ash

Triggers

Mum bumps Faye's pushchair up the council office steps. Thud, thud.
I'm glad because I can't hear her teeth grind. The same receptionist
as last time asks if Mum has an appointment. Mum's not clairvoyant.
The Somali security guard swings **By now she's unravelling hopes for**
a key fob thurible, pacing the transept **changes in her circumstances.**
between staffed cubicles and reception **Her jaw mashes side-to-side**
asks again if I'm alright. There's no air. **It feels like everyone there is**
Twitchy youths skulked in from vapey vestibules **watching us. Still we**
are asked which service they require, take a **shamble in. I'm holding a**
numbered ticket and swell the queues. A toddler **book of the six morals**
back-heels a pushchair, blows spit bubbles **representing** *My Family* **:**
ceilingward. Nothing happens sequentially. *The Religious Period* **but**
Families share crisps, consult mobiles while **I feel a world apart from**
others enter confessionals, recite **this phase, or phrase. Still, I master**
their liturgies of damp walls, rent arrears, **tracts by rote, try to please.**
absent fathers. Hope for refuge. By the sign **[A gateway to some peace]**
'Unsafe windows' I queue for parking permits. **Time slows to a pestle of**
teeth. The receptionist suggests returning tomorrow. Mum's face turns
red, her jaw loosens to fire questions about how she is supposed to feed
her kids on four weeks with no money. Tells me *I'm leaving …*

You stop here. At least you'll get fed.

The House of Locked Windows

Inside the box is a large tear, collected a drip at a time from the children in his care
— Joelle Taylor

1. *O Kukeli Korri* : A Doll's House

The last children's home I'm sent to
hides beneath a suburban veneer. It houses
back-of-the-class-girls and small-time dealers
abandoned teens with no options and gangs

of yo-yo visitors. The Housemother
sits in a pristine office shuffling papers
lectures about the ills of fags and permed
hair. Her head nods a mass of coir matting.

She mimics mothering sounds, chirps about
the expense of feeding her succession
of pubescent cuckoos. Bitchy girls call newbies
'fresh meat' when they try the locked windows.

As a welcome, the Housefather likes you
to sit on his lap and call him daddy.

2. *Muk* : Exeat

The men outside the house of locked windows,
standing under streetlamps texting or sitting
in BMWs emitting drifts of dope, wait
for the girls who press their tits against the panes.

The men are invisible to passing neighbours
and the vinegar stroke girls who go with them –
Croydon facelifts, school uniforms rolled up
at the waist – become invisible too.

No one reports them for bunking school
or when their beds are empty at curfew.
The other girls are jealous, the housemother silent:
it's like they've gone on holiday or never existed.

And when the girls resurface bruised and haunted
they're locked inside their dry-eyed 'don't care' act.

3. *Duvva Divvus Shan Peev Parno Muller :*
The Day She Drank White Spirit

Curtained from the ward's tableau of broken
things and other people's emergencies
and mechanised soundscapes, her private drama
played out. She drifted; bubble-gum scent lost

in disinfectant top-notes, unsubtle mid-notes
of rubber sheet. The gurney safety bar half-
masted, inside, fifteen, serene, and dying,
Rowan, pursed blue lips on adult secrets.

I watched the stages of her descent: skin
mottling, eyes drawn into darkened sockets
refocussed on inner battles, leaving me
behind and useless, trying to pull her back

by cracking lame jokes. From somewhere beyond reach
she whispered revelations with art room breath:
*Painkillers don't kill my pain
and the sleeping pills
don't help me sleep it away.*

It was her first attempt.

Talking With a Mouth Full of Stars

I regret the omission of women poets from this book. This is simply due to the fact that Britain in the last fifteen years has not produced a woman poet of real stature.

– Geoffrey Summerfield

you do not see me
grow
stones
at the edge

imagine this midnight moment
look across the
ruddled city

In the corner
a dove

shot-down

I thought I was tough

lopped head
stiffens

Presented in sequence, this erasure poem uses a single page of first lines from an anthology *Worlds*, (ed.) Geoffrey Summerfield, p.282.

Dear Faye,

I'll give you my fondest memory to climb inside. It's warm and smells lived in. I'll give you a morning after a blues party, waking in a house with a steady pulse of lovers' rock and laughter. I'll give you my whisper *It takes a village to raise a child.* This is our village. For a while. You are there in a borrowed cot, top-to-tail with Stafford whose hair could not be cut until he spoke his first word. His head is pillowed in three years of locks. I am across the room watching you sleeping, your mouth open, limbs splayed like a pond skater balanced on water tension. I'm snugged in a double bed with five of your cousins. Their afros hold constellations of pink and yellow blanket fluff. No one stirs as downstairs the sound system is dismantled and bumped up from the basement to the encouragement of shouted jokes, unheeded instructions. Soon the clatter of pans and plates, the sweet smell of plantain, dumplings and bacon frying will smother the ganga, last night's weed party. Uncle Calvin, who isn't our uncle, will smear a knife to spiced rust with hot pepper sauce, pepping himself up from the Guinness punch. Auntie Daphne, who isn't our auntie, will poke her stiff cloche of relaxed hair round the door, to ask if anybody is hungry. But for now, just listen to the juicy sound of our Mum singing;

Doctor Kitch, it's terrible, I can't stand the size of your needle.

Doctor Kitch, by Lord Kitchener

26

Places I've Nashed From

Immuring found text Philip Nikolayev, interviewed in The Argotist Online

Fetishized into a Romantic cult – the dynamics of which cannot be known
in advance – we command a kind of love to explore and intimately intern-
alise. Courtship as a breath unit, easy and inviting. I get into it too deeply
The first won't count as I was caught, half-in 'by the seat of one's pants'
half-out of Grandad's lavvy window, stuck to mount open-endedness …
on the sill flouting Race Day rules, his pigeons plumed with pitch. Some
flying home to roost. Sadly, absconding will surprise me, vivid musings,
from my first state home can't count as it was Malevich's Black Square
masterminded by my Mum – honestly an end result as lyric abandonment.
though, she was only interested in Outgrowing reactionary ideas to breed,
my sister. But I've nashed from every marginalised newsprint, trash talk-
foster carer, except Linda in Saint ing lineage, I walk boldly – go where?
Leonards on Sea where gulls bickered along A juddered line written with
rooftops, who brushed my wild hair hiding the Ouija board aesthetics of
ringworm bald patches. The tally rises what often escapes notice! It isn't
with schools where I was bullied, plus one crap Yoga to find myself –
relationship, survived by going missing. between spurts and dry patches –
It's not a Romani thing. It's about being hemmed in. a Shiva eye of salt
to click sharply into focus. With a straight face I lay bare to mine love, both
historic and chivalric, deconstruct their taste with tongue-in-cheek to be the
reliable or unreliable narrator with an instinctive reluctance to be

immured.

Dear Faye,

What did you see in your night terrors, staring into the oak-ink land-scapes leaked from your night-thoughts? You shattered nights with your bat voice, looked through or past us to something we dared not see. Did your duppy father barb you like a wasp while your mind roamed the dream-fields? Does his sting-soul hold fast in the bud of your mind, keep you half with him? We tethered you, like a kite, with a red chord tied at your index finger, kept it from pointing the *patrin* of a path to the dead world. It fixed the seep of your wandering outline. In the *muna-yak-oras* I have demons of my own. I'll mend myself with a red ribbon, write myself free with an alchemy of oak galls, crushed eggshells, Gum Arabic and dripped

honey.

Patrin: leaf, page and wayside signs; *muna-yak-oras*: moon hours; *FeS*: ferrous sulphate

Mi Loki Gili : My Song of Life

I practice the language my grandparents forgot
in a van, my *vardo*, parked in an *atchin tan* –
a layby far from fields, my off-grid home.
When the *gorja* retreated to their brick houses,
I lost the stigma of being an outsider.
In the hush, I only heard songbirds.
The city paused for the longest moment,
its soul grew calmer, the air grew cleaner,
and I stopped running just to stop looking backward.

I learned new words, limos : acceptance, smirom : peace.

To stop looking backward I just stopped running and
my soul grew calmer as the air grew cleaner.
For the longest moment, the city paused;
in the hush, I only heard songbirds.
I lost the stigma of being an outsider,
retreated from the *gorja* in their brick houses.
I lay by fields, my off-grid home, a Rom, far
in an *atchin tan*. In a parked van, my *vardo,*
I practice the language my grandparents forgot.

Vardo: home, wagon, caravan; *Atchin tan*: stopping place, safe place to stay;
Gorja: non-gypsy.

Acknowledgements

I would like to thank David Caddy for his workshops and tireless encouragement of new poetry. Thanks also to Tim Liardet, Rebecca 'Rebs' Althaus, Christopher Heath, Alun Hughes, Matt Coles, Oliver Wheater, and *The Work Shoppers* at the Anthony Anaxagorou and Richard Price Poetry School sessions who saw early versions of these poems and made it easier to share difficult subjects. Much appreciation also goes to Steve, Yola, Portia and Fifi for supplying coffee and love and my sisters, Faye and Terri, for our twisty history. Many thanks also to Ann and Peter Sansom and Ruth Padel for their faith in my work, and to Sarah Howe for her support, insight, and joyful laughter.

Thanks also to the editors of the following magazines and anthologies where the poems, or early versions of them, have appeared: *Wild Court, The North, The 87 Press, Tears in the Fence, Wagtail : The Roma Women's Poetry Anthology, How it Started the Creative Future Anthology, Not Very Quiet, Lucky Jefferson, Alyss Literary Journal, The Handy UnCapped Pen,* and *Ink Sweat and Tears.* 'A Confluence of Reds and Silks' won first place in the Cosmo Davenport-Hines Poetry Competition, 2021 and 'Framed by Woodgrain' was awarded a silver prize in the Creative Future competition, 2022.